Martial Arts
Karate
Kicks

by Stuart Schwartz
and Craig Conley

Consultant:
Mark Willie, Instructor
Central Minnesota Karate
Mankato State University

C A P S T O N E
H I G H / L O W B O O K S
an imprint of Capstone Press
Mankato, Minnesota

Capstone High/Low Books are published by Capstone Press
818 North Willow Street • Mankato, MN 56001
http://www.capstone-press.com

Library of Congress Cataloging-in-Publication Data
Schwartz, Stuart, 1945–
Karate kicks/by Stuart Schwartz and Craig Conley.
p. cm.—(Martial arts)
Includes bibliographical references (p. 44) and index.
Summary: A general description of karate, including its origins and
development, warm-up exercises, basic and advanced kicks, and safety
aspects.
ISBN 0-7368-0009-3
1. Karate—Juvenile literature. [1. Karate.] I. Conley, Craig, 1965– . II. Title.
III. Series: Martial arts (Mankato, Minn.)
GV1114.3.S356   1999
796.815—dc21
                                                    98-18589
                                                        CIP
                                                        AC

Editorial Credits
Cara Van Voorst, editor; James Frankin, cover designer and illustrator;
  Sheri Gosewisch, photo researcher

Photo Credits
All photographs by Gallery 19/Gregg R. Andersen.

Table of Contents

Chapter 1

Karate: A Martial Art

Karate is a form of self-defense in which the hands and feet are used as weapons. Self-defense is the act of protecting oneself. Karate means empty hand in Japanese. Karate students use a set of movements to protect themselves. The movements consist of blocks, strikes, punches, and kicks.

Karate-ka are karate students. Almost anyone can practice karate. Karate is a very physical activity. It can strain the heart and muscles. People should check with their doctors before they start to train.

The Beginning of Karate

Karate is a martial art. A martial art is a style of self-defense or fighting. Many martial arts

Karate is a form of self-defense that uses the hands and feet as weapons.

come from Asia. People on Okinawa Island near Japan developed karate in the 1600s. People in different areas soon developed their own styles of karate. There are more than 50 karate styles today. The movements described in this book are Shotokan style.

Many people call Gichin Funakoshi the Father of Modern Karate. He developed the Shotokan style of karate. Funakoshi performed a demonstration of his style for the Emperor of Japan. The emperor asked Funakoshi to open a karate school in 1922.

Funakoshi taught his Shotokan style of karate to many Japanese people until his death in 1957. Many karate schools still teach the Shotokan karate style today.

People in North America first learned karate from a sensei (SEN-say) named Oshima. Sensei means teacher in Japanese. People in North America liked karate as a sport. Today, many karate-ka participate in karate competitions. Students test their skills against other karate-ka at karate competitions.

A karate-ka moves his body to the correct position while looking in a mirror.

Places to Practice

Many cities throughout the world have dojos. A dojo is a karate school. A dojo has a wide, open room with mirrors. Karate-ka need the open room to perform basic karate movements. They can watch their movements in the mirrors. This helps karate-ka move their bodies to the correct positions.

People can practice karate anywhere there is open space. Some karate-ka practice karate outside or in large rooms at their homes.

Karate Kicks

Karate kicks are movements karate-ka use to attack or defend. Kicking movements can be difficult to learn. A karate-ka must have good balance to kick effectively. A student's weight is supported by only one leg when kicking. But properly performed kicks are very powerful.

A karate-ka needs to keep many things in mind when kicking. He should push his hips forward when kicking. This movement adds power to a kick. He also needs to remember to withdraw his kicking foot immediately after completing a kick. Otherwise, an opponent may grab his leg and pull him off balance during a fight.

A karate-ka must have good balance to kick effectively.

Chapter 2

Preparing to Train

Karate-ka practice only after they have warmed up. Karate-ka warm up to prepare their muscles for practice. They can hurt their muscles if they do not warm up. An injury may keep a karate-ka out of practice for weeks.

Karate students practice in loose-fitting clothing. Most karate-ka practice in gi (GEE). A gi is a loose-fitting cotton uniform. It has a belt that ties around the waist. Karate-ka receive different colored belts as they master certain skills. Beginning karate-ka wear white belts. The most advanced karate-ka wear black belts.

Karate-ka do leg stretches before practicing kicks. Good leg stretches include standing leg

Most karate-ka practice in gi.

stretches, step switches, and hip and knee rotations. A rotation is a circular motion made by a body part. These stretches prepare waist and leg muscles for practice.

Standing Leg Stretches

A karate-ka stands straight up to begin a standing leg stretch. His feet are two shoulder widths apart. His toes are pointed forward. He then slowly bends to the left and holds his left ankle with his left hand. He locks his left knee.

Next the karate-ka places his right hand on his lower left leg. He pulls his body to his left leg and holds it there for about 10 seconds. Then he stands up and does the same movements on his right side.

Step Switches

Step switches increase hip and leg coordination. Coordination is the ability of body parts to work together. A karate-ka begins a step switch from a natural stance. The natural stance begins with one leg forward. This stance is similar to a walking stance.

A karate-ka pulls his body to his leg during a standing leg stretch.

The karate-ka jumps from a right natural stance to a left natural stance. She keeps her feet as close to the ground as possible. Then she jumps back to the right natural stance again.

Hip and Knee Rotations

Hip rotations stretch hip and waist muscles. A karate-ka begins a hip rotation with his feet shoulder width apart. The karate-ka places his hands on his hips and rotates his hips in a circular motion. He rotates his hips to the right. He then rotates his hips to the left.

Karate-ka do knee rotations to loosen and strengthen their knees. A karate-ka begins a knee rotation with his feet together and his knees bent forward. He places his hands on his knees. He rotates his knees to the right. He then rotates his knees to the left.

Karate-ka perform knee rotations to loosen and strengthen their knees.

Chapter 3

Basic Kicks

There are two basic motions used in karate kicks. They are snapping and thrusting motions. Snap kicks are very quick movements. Thrust kicks are more powerful movements. A karate-ka decides which kick will work best for each situation.

A karate-ka keeps his knees relaxed for a snap kick. First he bends and raises his knee. Then he snaps his foot out and quickly withdraws it.

A karate-ka begins a thrust kick with his knee bent and raised. Then he pushes his leg outward. He pushes his hips forward at the same time. This motion increases the power of the kick.

A karate-ka begins a thrust kick with his knee bent and raised.

Straddle-leg Stance

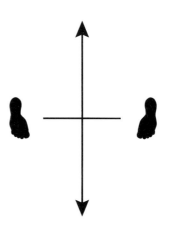

Front Stance

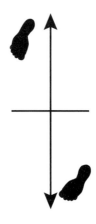

18

There are four basic kicks used in karate. They are the front kick, side kick, round kick, and back kick. The front kick and side kick can be either snap kicks or thrust kicks. The round kick is a snap kick. The back kick is a thrust kick. Each kick can be performed with either the right leg or the left leg. This book describes kicks performed with the right leg.

Stances

Stances are the basis of every movement in karate. A karate-ka learns proper stances from the beginning of his or her karate training. A karate-ka can deliver a kick from most stances. Two common stances are the straddle-leg stance and front stance.

In the straddle-leg stance, a karate-ka's legs are out to the sides. His feet are about two shoulder widths apart. His feet point forward. His knees are slightly outward and bent forward. His knees do not bend past his feet.

In a front stance, a karate-ka keeps her front knee bent and her back leg straight. The knee of her front leg is directly over her front foot.

Start

Finish

A karate-ka uses a side thrust kick when she wants a powerful kick.

Side Kicks

The side kick also can have either a snapping or a thrusting motion. A side kick is very similar to a front kick. A karate-ka can begin a side kick from a straddle-leg stance. A karate-ka bends and raises her right knee to begin a right side snap kick. But she moves her knee 45 degrees to the side.

The karate-ka then snaps her lower leg out to the side and quickly withdraws it. She aims at the target with the outer edge of her foot.

There are four basic kicks used in karate. They are the front kick, side kick, round kick, and back kick. The front kick and side kick can be either snap kicks or thrust kicks. The round kick is a snap kick. The back kick is a thrust kick. Each kick can be performed with either the right leg or the left leg. This book describes kicks performed with the right leg.

Stances

Stances are the basis of every movement in karate. A karate-ka learns proper stances from the beginning of his or her karate training. A karate-ka can deliver a kick from most stances. Two common stances are the straddle-leg stance and front stance.

In the straddle-leg stance, a karate-ka's legs are out to the sides. His feet are about two shoulder widths apart. His feet point forward. His knees are slightly outward and bent forward. His knees do not bend past his feet.

In a front stance, a karate-ka keeps her front knee bent and her back leg straight. The knee of her front leg is directly over her front foot.

Start

Finish

A karate-ka snaps her foot forward from her knee during a front snap kick.

Her feet are shoulder width apart. She keeps her back straight. The karate-ka can face her upper body forward or turn it to the side.

Front Kicks

Many karate-ka begin a front kick from a front stance. Front kicks can be either snapping or thrusting kicks. A karate-ka moves her right hip forward and raises her right knee to begin a right front snap kick. She then snaps her foot

Start

Finish

A karate-ka uses the muscles in his thigh to thrust his foot out to the target during a front thrust kick.

forward from the knee. She pulls her toes backward. She strikes at the target with the ball of her foot. The ball of the foot is the area at the base of the toes. After she hits the target, she quickly withdraws her foot.

A karate-ka begins a right front thrust kick the same way as the front snap kick. But he thrusts his leg out from the thigh instead of snapping from his knee. He strikes the target with either the ball of his foot or his heel.

Start

Finish

A karate-ka uses a side thrust kick when she wants a powerful kick.

Side Kicks

The side kick also can have either a snapping or a thrusting motion. A side kick is very similar to a front kick. A karate-ka can begin a side kick from a straddle-leg stance. A karate-ka bends and raises her right knee to begin a right side snap kick. But she moves her knee 45 degrees to the side.

The karate-ka then snaps her lower leg out to the side and quickly withdraws it. She aims at the target with the outer edge of her foot.

Start

Finish

Most karate-ka use the round kick to hit the head or chest areas of opponents.

A karate-ka begins a right side thrust kick by raising her right knee in front of her chest. Then she pushes the leg out to the side. She locks her knee and aims at the target with the outer edge of her foot.

The Round Kick

Most karate-ka use the round kick to hit the head or chest areas of opponents. A round kick can start from a front stance. A karate-ka uses the right back leg to perform a round kick. The round kick is a snap kick. A karate-ka begins a right round kick by rotating his hips forward. He moves his right leg forward and raises his back leg. He bends his knee and raises it to hip level. His upper leg is even with the ground.

The karate-ka then turns to his left. He snaps his lower leg forward when his leg is close to the target. He pulls his toes up and hits the target with the ball of his foot. The karate-ka then quickly withdraws his leg.

The Back Kick

A back kick is a thrust kick. Many karate-ka use back kicks when opponents approach from behind. Sometimes karate-ka turn and back kick targets in front of them.

A karate-ka begins a right back kick standing straight with his feet together. The karate-ka lifts his right leg. The knee of his leg is bent in front of him. Then he leans his body slightly forward and straightens his knee behind him. The karate-ka hits the target with his heel. He looks over his right shoulder while he is kicking to spot the target.

A back kick is a thrust kick.

Start

Finish: Back View

Finish: Side View

Chapter 4

Advanced Kicks

Karate-ka who master basic kicks can learn advanced kicks. Advanced kicks include crescent kicks and jumping kicks. Crescent kicks use a sweeping motion. Karate-ka perform jumping kicks while in the air.

Crescent Kicks
Karate-ka use crescent kicks to hit opponents' head, chest, or groin areas. A karate-ka can aim a crescent kick to the front or to the side. Skilled karate-ka also can block punches with crescent kicks. Some karate-ka use reverse crescent kicks.

A karate-ka begins a right front crescent kick from a front stance. His right leg is back. He swings his right leg in a circular motion to

A karate-ka can aim a crescent kick to the front.

the left side. He swings it in, across, and downward in a half-circle.

A karate-ka also can perform a reverse crescent kick. A karate-ka swings his right leg in and upward. He continues the kick in a sweeping motion away from the opposite side. The karate-ka hits a target in front of his body with the ball of his foot.

A right crescent kick to the side begins from the straddle-leg stance. A karate-ka swings his right leg out and upward in a sweeping motion. He hits his hand with the sole of his foot. Then he swings his leg downward and returns to the straddle-leg stance. A karate-ka holds his left hand out to the side with his palm facing forward.

Jumping Kicks

Only advanced students should practice jumping kicks. A karate-ka kicks his target while in the air during a jumping kick. His body's forward motion gives more power to the kick. A karate-ka adds a jump to a basic kick to perform a jumping kick. The jumping

A karate-ka swings his leg in and upward for a reverse crescent kick.

Start

Finish

Start

Middle

Finish

front kick and the jumping side kick are two jumping kicks.

A karate-ka practices only low jumping kicks at first. He gradually increases the height of his jump. He leans his upper body forward to maintain his balance while kicking.

A karate-ka begins a jumping right front kick from a front stance. He runs a short distance. He bends his left leg at his ankle, knee, and hip. Then he straightens and pushes off the ground with his left foot. His leg acts as a spring. It pushes his body upward. He kicks the target with his right foot. Both the front snap and front thrust kicks can be jumping kicks.

The karate-ka uses the same movements for the jumping side kick. The jumping side kick is usually a thrust kick. A karate-ka begins a left jumping side kick from the front stance. He shifts his weight to his right leg and pushes off the ground with that leg. He brings his right heel toward his inner thigh. He thrusts his left leg out and downward at the same time. He hits the target with the outer edge of his left foot.

The jumping side kick is usually a thrust kick.

Students must listen when the instructor speaks. Karate-ka sit or stand at attention and listen to the instructor.

Instructors at all karate dojos take steps to make sure their students stay safe. Instructors have rules about grooming, warming up, conditioning, and controlling movements. They also make sure karate-ka wear protective gear.

Grooming

Grooming is taking care of appearance and clothing. Karate-ka need to keep their bodies and uniforms clean. This is important because sweat and dirt can cause illness.

Karate-ka must keep their fingernails and toenails trimmed. Long nails can scratch people. Karate-ka also tie back long hair for practice. They might not see a kick or strike if they have hair in their faces.

Karate-ka remove their watches and jewelry before practicing. Jewelry could hurt the karate-ka or others during practice. Karate-ka could be kicked in the ear and an earring could pierce their skin. Or a watch could scratch another student.

Chapter 5

Safety and Training

Safety is an important part of karate training. Shotokan karate-ka practice low-contact karate. These students practice in light-contact or in no-contact situations.

Some karate dojos offer high-contact styles of karate. Karate-ka at these dojos practice in full-contact situations. Karate-ka have a greater chance of hurting themselves during high-contact practice.

Karate students learn to respect their instructors and other students as part of their training. They bow to show respect. Karate-ka bow to their instructors before and after class. Sparring opponents bow to each other before and after a match. Sparring is practice fighting.

Safety is an important part of karate training.

Students must listen when the instructor speaks. Karate-ka sit or stand at attention and listen to the instructor.

Instructors at all karate dojos take steps to make sure their students stay safe. Instructors have rules about grooming, warming up, conditioning, and controlling movements. They also make sure karate-ka wear protective gear.

Grooming

Grooming is taking care of appearance and clothing. Karate-ka need to keep their bodies and uniforms clean. This is important because sweat and dirt can cause illness.

Karate-ka must keep their fingernails and toenails trimmed. Long nails can scratch people. Karate-ka also tie back long hair for practice. They might not see a kick or strike if they have hair in their faces.

Karate-ka remove their watches and jewelry before practicing. Jewelry could hurt the karate-ka or others during practice. Karate-ka could be kicked in the ear and an earring could pierce their skin. Or a watch could scratch another student.

front kick and the jumping side kick are two jumping kicks.

A karate-ka practices only low jumping kicks at first. He gradually increases the height of his jump. He leans his upper body forward to maintain his balance while kicking.

A karate-ka begins a jumping right front kick from a front stance. He runs a short distance. He bends his left leg at his ankle, knee, and hip. Then he straightens and pushes off the ground with his left foot. His leg acts as a spring. It pushes his body upward. He kicks the target with his right foot. Both the front snap and front thrust kicks can be jumping kicks.

The karate-ka uses the same movements for the jumping side kick. The jumping side kick is usually a thrust kick. A karate-ka begins a left jumping side kick from the front stance. He shifts his weight to his right leg and pushes off the ground with that leg. He brings his right heel toward his inner thigh. He thrusts his left leg out and downward at the same time. He hits the target with the outer edge of his left foot.

The jumping side kick is usually a thrust kick.

Students must pay attention when the instructor speaks.

Warming Up and Conditioning

Karate-ka warm up before they practice.
Karate-ka stretch their muscles to help prevent
injuries. Karate-ka might pull muscles if they
do not warm up.

Conditioning is exercising daily to keep the
body fit. Some karate-ka lift weights and jog
to condition themselves. These exercises
strengthen their hearts, muscles, and lungs.

Karate-ka who are fit are less likely to accidentally hurt themselves. They can practice karate longer without becoming tired. Tired karate-ka can become careless. Careless karate-ka might do movements wrong and hurt themselves. Or they might lose control of a movement and accidentally hurt someone else.

Sparring

Many karate-ka train so they can spar. Two karate-ka compete in a sparring match. Judges award karate-ka points during sparring matches. The person who scores the most points wins the match. Karate-ka must follow rules for sparring. Karate sparring rules are meant to keep karate-ka safe.

Some students prefer no-contact or light-contact sparring. They try to keep their kicks from hitting their opponents in this kind of sparring. They try to stop their kicks within one inch (2.5 centimeters) of their opponents. Other styles of karate use high-contact sparring. Karate-ka make contact in this kind

Many karate-ka train so they can spar.

of sparring. But these students still need to control their movements. They are not allowed to hit their opponents in the face. They must aim for body areas that are protected by pads.

A karate-ka learns to control her movements as part of her training. She controls her movements so she does not hurt herself or other students. She might twist her arm or leg the wrong way if she does a movement improperly. Or she might accidentally hit another person.

Protective Gear

Tournament officials require karate-ka to wear protective gear when they spar. Karate-ka wear mouth guards and padded gloves during a sparring match. A mouth guard protects the teeth. A kick or punch to the mouth could break or knock out unprotected teeth. Padded gloves cover the hands and fingers up to the knuckles. The gloves protect the hands while blocking or punching.

Tournament officials require karate-ka to wear protective gear when they spar.

Students who prefer high-contact sparring need additional protective gear. They may wear helmets, chest protectors, forearm guards, shin guards, and foot pads. This padded gear protects body parts from hits. It also protects karate-ka's arms, legs, hands, and feet when they hit opponents or hard surfaces.

Karate is an exciting sport to learn. But it can be dangerous if people do not follow the rules. Beginning students should not try to perform advanced movements before they master basic movements. Advanced students should continue to practice basic movements. Practice and patience will help karate-ka develop karate skills safely.

Practice and patience will help karate-ka develop karate skills safely.

Words to Know

competition (kom-puh-TISH-uhn)—a contest of skill

condition (kuhn-DISH-uhn)—to exercise daily to keep the body fit

dojo (DOH-joh)—a karate school

gi (GEE)—a loose-fitting, cotton uniform

groom (GROOM)—to take care of appearance and clothing

injury (IN-juh-ree)—harm to the body

martial art (MAR-shuhl ART)—a style of self-defense and fighting; many martial arts come from Asia

rotation (roh-TAY-shuhn)—a circular motion made by a body part

self-defense (SELF-di-FENSS)—the act of protecting oneself

sparring (SPAHR-ing)—practice fighting

Karate-ka learn skills for self-defense.

To Learn More

Corrigan, Ralph. *Karate Made Easy.* New York: Sterling Publications, 1995.

Gutman, Bill. *Karate.* Minneapolis: Capstone Press, 1995.

Leder, Jane Mersky. *Karate.* Learning How. Marco, Fla.: Bancroft-Sage Publishing, 1992.

Queen, J. Allen. *Start Karate!* New York: Sterling Publications, 1997.

Sieh, Ron. *Martial Arts for Beginners.* New York: Writers and Readers, 1995.

Karate-ka learn to defend against attackers.

Useful Addresses

Canadian Shotokan Karate Association
1646 McPherson Drive
Port Coquitlam, BC V3C 6C9
Canada

**International Society for
  Okinawan/Japanese Karate**
21512 Sherman Way
Canoga Park, CA 91303

Shotokan Karate of America
2500 South La Cienega Boulevard
Los Angeles, CA 90034

World Federation Karate Organization
9506 Las Tunas Drive
Temple City, CA 91780

Internet Sites

Canadian Shotokan Karate Association
http://www.geocities.com/colosseum/field/
  7270

Martial Arts Resource Page
http://www.middlebury.edu/~jswan/
  martial.arts/ma.html

Shotokan Karate for Everyone
http://members.aol.com/edl12/shotokan/
  index.htm

Shotokan Karate of America
http://www.ska.org/

Index